Myths, Monsters & Love From The South of Chile

Thomas Jerome Baker

ISBN: 978 1511686679
ISBN-13: 1511686677

DEDICATION

"Delightful Dreams", is dedicated to young and old alike. It is a centuries-old myth that has been passed down from generation to generation on the island of Chiloé. This island is located in the extreme southern sector of Chile, far from the urban center of the country.

This fact partly explains the fertile ground available for the myth's survival to the present day. More importantly, its context is a superstitious world that sought to explain the mysteries of the natural world through the medium of dreams and myths. In fact, according to Joseph Campbell, "Myths are public dreams, dreams are private myths."

"People say that what we're all seeking is a meaning for life. I don't think that's what we're really seeking. I think that what we're seeking is an experience of being alive, so that our life experiences on the purely physical plane will have resonances with our own innermost being and reality, so that we actually feel the rapture of being alive."
~ Joseph Campbell, "The Power of Myth".

CONTENTS

ACKNOWLEDGMENTS

I am indebted to literally thousands of storytellers who kept this story "alive", orally, through the centuries of recorded time. In this way, it has come to me. Now, after living fifteen years in Chile, I have acquired the cultural capital necessary to tell this story in written form.

To be clear, I first encountered this story in the same way that most travelers to the island of Chiloé do, in oral form. Someone, who had heard the story told, kept the oral tradition alive by retelling the story to me. In turn, I now "tell" the story to you.

It is a story best appreciated when told with the human voice. As an instrument of drama, tension, and apprehension, the human voice has no equal. As you tell the story, your "voice" will emerge.

So, as you read the story, feel free to make vivid use of your imagination. It is a time and place when there were things in the natural world which defied man's ability to comprehend. Thus, out of necessity, the myth was employed to bridge the gap. The "vehicle" which is best used to travel over the "bridge" is of course, your "voice".

I hope you enjoy reading, telling, and retelling this story.

CHAPTER ONE

SUMMER VACATION

As I remember it, October, 2003 was coming to a close. Gaby and I had been married for six spectacular months. Spectacular, because we were deeply in love, one mind and one heart existing in two human bodies. You know what I mean, right? Gaby would say something, and I would finish her sentence. Or I would look at something, and she would speak my thoughts before I even had time to think of what it was that I was going to say. As I said, we were deeply in love.

Anyway, on this particular day I was reading the newspaper. I had just finished the sports section, my favorite part of the newspaper in those days. At that time, football in Chile was undergoing a period of radical change. The unthinkable had happened.

Colo Colo, one of the most successful and most popular teams in Chile, declared bankruptcy in January, 2002. The team was approximately 30 Million US dollars in debt, and unable to pay. Consequently, there was a high risk that the team would disappear completely from the ranks of professional football.

To avoid the same nightmarish scenario, most teams eventually reorganized themselves from non-profit corporations or institutions into for-profit status. This was legally possible due to a law which would take effect in 2005, Law 20.019 "Sociedades Anónimas Deportivas" (SADP). As a for-profit entity, the survival of the teams would now be due to market oriented reasons. Football in Chile was now privatized, a business just like any other.

At the same time, the Chilean Football Association (ANFP) decided to innovate in order to make "The Beautiful Game", as football is known, more profitable. The annual competition was changed into a competition having two championships per year, with a system of playoffs to determine the champion.

This was an imitation of the Mexican model. By contrast, the previous system had been a longer contest based on home and away matches, with the team accumulating the highest number of points by season end being declared the champion. There were no playoffs.

In 2002, the first champion under this new model was

Universidad Católica. In the final, they defeated Rangers, the team from Talca. In the second tournament of the year, lo and behold, Colo Colo was once again champion. They had done it with a team of young but hungry players, and only a handful of veterans, notably Marcelo Espina and Marcelo Barticciotto. They defeated Universidad Católica, who was coached by Juvenal Olmos. Juvenal would go on to coach the national team the following year.

A final note is in order before returning to our tale. Some 8 years later, on April 18, 2013, an article in the "La Tercera" newspaper would solemnly report the following: "The majority of the teams organized under the SADP Law have failed. The law was intended to save the football teams. It didn't happen. The big teams (Colo Colo, Universidad de Chile, Universidad Católica) owe twice as much now as they did 8 years ago. 85% of the professional teams are bankrupt." It seems "Big Business" had not been the answer.

Anyway, as I finished reading the paper, "The Beautiful Game" was as exciting as ever. The top teams were scrambling to maintain their form and enter the playoffs in the best possible position for the early rounds. It looked like Universidad Católica was in a very good position to win the championship for the second time.

Contentedly, I turned from the sports section to the vacation and travel section. Then I saw it. Before I could say what I was thinking, Gaby spoke for me, telling me what I was thinking.

"The South of Chile would be a nice vacation. Lake Llanquihue, Lake Todos Los Santos, Puerto Montt, Puerto Varas, Frutillar, Osorno, Valdivia, and Chiloé."

"Yes, let's book it now while it is a steal", I replied immediately.

I could have saved my breath. Gaby was already on the phone talking to the travel agent. I turned my head and looked out the window. Although it was a mild, overcast day, with a grayish tint over everything, I was seeing a beautiful, bright, sunny summer day. In my mind's eye there was warmth and laughter, lazy days with nothing to do but enjoy the passage of time in the company of the most special person on Earth, my Gaby.

"One hundrd eighty thousand pesos. You have to pay forty

thousand pesos to hold the reservation. Unless you pay the fee, they won't hold your reservation if someone else wants it."

Gaby's voice brught me back to reality as she repeated her words to me. I noticed it was beginning to rain outside.

"Where was I going to get forty thousand pesos from, let alone 180 thousand pesos?", I thought to myself.

"Didn't Gaby know I was a school teacher, living from paycheck to paycheck? Does she think I've got money in the bank?"

Flashback:
The day is Saturday, April 6, 2002. The church is full of family, relatives, and friends. A few curious onlookers are on hand, pleased to witness the event. A long, white limousine pulls up in front of the church. A beautiful woman in a long, white, wedding dress steps out of the limo.

Inside the church, I'm nervous. I've never been so nervous in my life. I've made it to the church only 10 minutes before the arrival of the limo. Yes, I was almost late for my wedding. Almost. Juan, my cousin and chauffeur, seems to have an intimate knowledge of every side street in Santiago. With a tranquility that was maddening, he has brought me here in the nick of time.

The music begins to play. If you've heard it once, you've heard it a thousand times. Yes, I've heard it a thousand times. Only now, it's playing for me. And here she comes, down the aisle. Bernardo is to her right, escorting his sister to be married. He is standing in for his father, who had passed away last year.

They reach me, the music stops, and Bernardo places Gaby's hand in mine. She looks at me, and I don't even recognize her. I've never seen this woman before in my life, not this woman.

"Who is this woman? Are you going to be my wife? Look, let's not tell Gaby about this...and then she smiles at me.

It's Gaby!

"Oh My God, what happened to you? You are the most beautiful woman in

5

the world! And I'm getting married to you? Wow! I'm the luckiest man in the world!

Now I'm sitting in the limo, married, by now totally convinced that Gaby has a fairy godmother. Six white mice have been converted into this white limo, Gaby has been transformed into a queen, and me?

I dare not look at her feet. If she's wearing glass slippers, this dream of complete and total happiness will come to an end at midnight. The limo will turn back into mice, Gaby will go back to her old life as a servant girl. And me? I'll be left holding a glass slipper.

Midnight comes and goes. Gaby is real, becoming more radiantly beautiful as the night goes on until the wee hours of the morning. We dance the night away, the most magnificent night of my entire life.

The limo does not change, Gaby's shoes are white (not glass), and what about me?

I'm the King of the World, the whole world. What a wonderful world, as Louis Armstrong would say. I couldn't agree more...

CHAPTER TWO

YAN KEE WAY (Llanquihue)

It's the middle of January, 2003. Gaby and I have finally arrived in Puerta Varas. We are staying in a cabin only 5 minutes walking distance from Lake Llanquihue. Our package includes breakfast, but lunch and dinner is not included. That leaves us free to find interesting restaurants to eat dinner at. For lunch, we will economise by shopping for snacks at the local shops and food vendors.

Our vacation package is one that will have us very busy. With our headquarters in Puerta Varas, we will be taking tours by bus practically every day. In this way, we will be able to see an incredible number of places that would be impossible for us to see otherwise.

Puerto Varas is on the shore of Lake Llanquihue. It is an adventure travel hub and the gateway to Vicente Pérez National Park. It is a beautiful town, situated on a major lake. It has quaint architecture and a vibrant, bustling center. It has a casino, many tour operators, and a flow of tourists that does not quite make it to the overcrowded category. Since the weather is unpredictable, many tourists bypass Puerto Varas for Pucón, where the weather is more predictable.

The city was founded by German immigrants and later became an important shipping point for goods being shipped to Puerto Montt. The city relies heavily on tourism, but it is also a residential community for people who work in Puerto Montt. While Gaby and I were there, we would see Puerto Varas only by the light of the moon or in the early morning. We were always on the move by day.

We went on daily sightseeing tours around the Lake District. Each day a new destination, a new door, a new place, a new face. Frutillar, Puerto Montt, The Fish Market of Angelmó, Lago Todos Los Santos, Osorno, Calbuco, Puyehue, Saltos de Petrohue (Petrohue Falls), Chacao, Ancud, Valdivia, Parque Nacional Vicente Pérez Rosales, and three volcanoes: Osorno, Tronador, and Puntiagudo. The park is open from 9am to 8pm in the summer.

By far one of the highlights of the trip was the visit to Calbuco. Our destination was the Chaullín Island (Isla Chaullín), where Gaby and I had the opportunity to eat "Curanto" and dance Cueca on an island with a rich history of prohibited love. But let me begin at the beginning.

What is Curanto and what is Cueca? Well, the national dance of Chile is called the Cueca. I was taught to dance cueca by my mother in law, Julia Vargas. Seeing as how Gaby and I planned to celebrate the customs and traditions of Chile when we got married, she thought I might as well learn how to dance a proper Cueca.

It seems the Cueca is similar to the mating ritual of the rooster and the hen. Basically, the rooster follows the hen, who appears to be well within the reach of the rooster. Somehow, the rooster never catches the hen, but follows her back and forth across the yard, until finally, the hen decides she wants to be caught. It's a dance which has regional variations, just as there are regional variations of speech.

Oh, Curanto? Well, yes, it is delicious. How do you make it? You dig a big hole in the ground, throw in some hot stones, cover that up with leaves, throw in potatoes, sausages and meat, cover that up until everything is heated up nicely. Remove the big leaves, pull out the meat and potatoes, and enjoy. Now, this is not quite precise, but the general idea is on target.

Flashback:

It's the early 1800's, and Emil Whilenhausen, a Swiss immigrant, is the first owner of the island. To this island he brings his lover, who is 25 years younger than him. They give the island the name of "Helvecia". As the years go by, Emil plants exotic plants and native trees, turning the island into a paradisical landscape with a spectacular forest. For the locals, the island has become an iconic place which symbolizes innocence and youth. Not a trace remains of Emil and his young lover, unless you find an amazing sculpted tree.

I found such a tree, in the form of a woman. When I asked one of the musicians who played the music at our festival that day, he looked at me oddly, and said: "You found her."

Yes, I had found her, but who was she? There would be no answer from the musician. As I looked at the photo after having it developed, I began to ask people if they might know. It was an old fisherman, in the Angelmó Fish Market, who would finally provide the answer.

"La Pincoya. It's La Pincoya, the Goddess of Fertility of the Sea. She is responsible for all living things in the sea."

"What else can you tell me about her?"

"She is responsible for the abundance or the scarcity of fish and seafood. When she rises from the depths of the ocean each morning, and begins her dance, with her arms extended to the sea, it will be a good day. The catch will be generous. But if La Pincoya faces the coast, the fish will have left the area. They will be gone because she has decided to move the fish to another area. To have good luck, one must be happy, positive and cooperative. Also, it is important to rotate the areas where you fish, or La Pincoya will be angry."

With that, the old man went on his way, leaving me the wiser for his words. I could see why he had told me. Although I was no fisherman, he knew that I would not place much faith in the idea of a mermaid rising from the water each day. That was fantastical thinking, which put your fate in the hands of an arbitrary creature with mythical powers. In this way, you were no longer responsible for the results of your efforts. Everything was a matter of destiny. Fate was either with you, or against you. That's quite fatalistic.

At the same time, the old man had left me with something that I could grasp intellectually. If you rotated your fishing "grounds" on a regular basis, you would be likely to avoid overfishing any one area. By moving frequently, each area would be able to regenerate itself, avoiding depletion. La Pincoya, the myth, promoted good values such as positive thinking, a good attitude, and a wilingness to cooperate with other fishermen. The myth served as a guiding construct which benefitted everyone involved with fishing.

As I thought back to the island of Chaullín, I wondered why such a figure would be found there, cut out of a tree. Slowly, I began to smile. I had it figured out.

La Pincoya was real. Serious people believed that a mermaid rose out of the sea every morning, possibly in the mist of the early morning, to dance on the water. When she would dance facing the sea, the catch would be abundant. If towards the coast, the message was clear: Go to another area. The fish have moved to another area where it is more necessary.

The belief in La Pincoya was so strong that this Goddess of the Fertility of the Sea had been constructed. Being only a short distance away from Calbuco (15 minutes), it would be easily seen by any eyes that were watching for a signal. Based on the sight of La Pincoya, the ultimate destination of the day's fishing would be determined.

Would it have been easier without La Pincoya? What is the role of myth in human society? Without the myth, is the life of the fisherman richer, or poorer? Joseph Campbell would probably say that the fisherman's life would be poorer. He believed that mythology was a cultural and societal construct that could not be divorced from the culture and environment it was a part of.

This knowledge would be instrumental in helping me to understand the major myth that I would come into contact with on the island of Chiloé. In this myth, delightful dreams play a role that is one of appearances, but not of reality. I come now to the subject of this book, the myth of "El Trauco".

By way of introduction, a poem by Dario Cavada C. comes to mind. Called, "El Trauco", it was written in 1926 for the centenario celebration of Chiloé (1826 – 1926).

EL TRAUCO

Do you really breathe? Are you only a myth? Why don't you come into the light of day? Why don't you let go with a mighty shout to the multitude? I want to try the delicious filter that puts the maiden to sleep. Cuasimodo Chilote, be pious! I want to see my beautiful one asleep. Stay put where you are, in the mysterious sleepy jungle. Outside of that world, there are no charms, no spells. Don't come, Trauco! Don't come to the city to trouble virginal hearts. Stay put where you are, in your vast solitude. Only the country fruit is what you deserve.

CHAPTER THREE

Chiloé, Myths & Legends

Welcome to Ancud. That's what the sign says. Gaby and I couldn't resist, so we got off the bus and took a pic standing beside the sign welcoming us to one of the major cities on the island of Chiloé. To be honest, after crossing over from the mainland by ferryboat, we were just glad to feel "Terra firma" under our feet again.

Before coming over, we had stopped to have lunch at Restaurant

Canal Chacao, near the dock where the ferryboat picks up and drops off passengers and vehicles. Gaby and I had fried salmon and rice. The pink meat had been deliciously tender, almost melting in my mouth. We shared a bottle of white wine between us with another couple who were traveling with us. It had been a delicious meal after the long bus ride up from Puerto Varas.

On the ferry we had watched the Chilean dolphins, called "toninas" leaping in the water and racing the ferry boat to the other side. With the bus on the ferry, we had taken places where we could get a good view of the ocean. It had been thrilling to watch the land mass of the mythical island Chiloé coming nearer and nearer.

Chiloé, land of mythical people and creatures. Chiloé, land of many churches. Two world views inhabiting the same space. That was the Chiloé I had expected to find, and I was not disappointed. Ancud is the northern entrance to the island of Chiloé.

While there, we visited the church in Ancud, called Catedral San Carlos de Ancud. After that, we visited Fort Antonio, which is an old Spanish fort. In fact, it was the last fort held by Spain in the War of Independence. After that we made our way to the plaza to do some shopping before our bus would be leaving to take us back to Puerta Varas, our home away from home.

Flashback:
Ancud was founded in 1768. The Governor of the Archipelago, Mr. Carlos Beranguer, gave the city the name of "Villa de San Carlos de Chiloé. This name was changed on the 4th of July, 1834, to its pesent day name, Ancud.

The Discovery of Chiloé
In February of 1540, Alonso de Camargo saw, before anyone else, the west coast of Chiloé. At that time, it was already known by the natives as *Chilhué*. However, the true discoverer of the Archipiélago was Capitán Don Francisco de Ulloa. In the year 1553, he made important explorations. Travelers following in his footsteps took advantage of his work.

Chiloé
" Durante toda su historia, los habitantes de Chiloé han recibido del exterior influencias culturales. Los conquistadores españoles, los

piratas, europeos, los misioneros, y aventureros en general han dejado su huella en la mentalidad chilota, que ha sabido integrar con armonía, fantasía y sueños, una realidad que muchas veces escapa de su propio universo creando un mundo íntimo que se palpa en el ambiente su fascinante atracción." (enigmas y otros misterios)

Chiloé is the second largest island in South America and the largest island of Chile. The island is located at the south end of Chile in the Lake District. The coastal mountains cross its entire length creating two completely different environments. Toward the Pacific, the coast receives constant damp winds from the ocean and heavy rainfalls, so there is abundant vegetation. Facing the continent, the island's microclimate allows for human life with all its folklore and varied mythology.

The province area is composed of three groups of islands: Chilo, Guaitecas, and Chonos. It extends from the narrow strait of Chacao to the Peninsula of Taytao. The population is composed mainly of Indians, distantly related to the tribes of the mainland and mestizos. The capital of the province is Ancud.

The Beginning

Chiloé begins its history hundreds of years before the arrival of the Spanish expeditions. The primitive inhabitants of the islands were Huilliches, Cuncos, and Chonos. They were a peaceful people who lived on hunting, fishing and harvesting. Twenty years after the discovery of the Strait of Magellan, Don Alonso de Camargo saw this group of islands but did not take possession of them. In 1558, a group of Spanish men under the leadership of Juan Gutierrez de Altamirano landed on the Big Island of Chiloé. Don Alonso de Ercilla refers to this fact as follows:

Al fin, una manana descubrimos
De Ancud el espacioso y fertile raso,
Y al pie del monte y aspera ladera
Un extendido lago y gran ribera. (Chiloé)

Nevertheless, the most important expedition arrived in the island in 1567 with 110 horsemen. From this time, different Spanish expeditions were sent to control the southern territories of the Realm of Chile.

In 1608, the Jesuits arrived. Their mission was to teach the gospel to the Indians and evangelize them. After almost 200 years, they were obliged to leave the territory and the Franciscans took their place. In 1600 and 1643 respectively, the island faced the invasion and attack from Dutch corsairs who wanted to find out where the Indians used to get gold. Though stories of a golden city, "La Ciudad Encantada" were widely told, in fact, no such golden city has ever been found on Chilean soil.

In 1826, Chiloé was the last territory annexed to the Chilean nation. In fact, after 10 years of the consolidation of the independence, there still were troops fighting in favor of Spain.

The different interests and efforts of the government to colonize this wild and isolated land became reality in 1895 when a group of Europeans from Great Britain, Germany, Poland, Italy, Austria, France ,and Russia settled in this new land.

"En la tarde del 22 de Septiembre de 1895, cuando poco, casi nada, se había alcanzado a preparar para su instalación, fondeaba en Ancud el vapor Tormés con los primeros colonos" (Chiloé).

Tales, Myths, and Legends

A myth is a story that has deep explanatory or symbolic resonance for a culture. All cultures have developed their own myths to explain their origin, history, religion, and heroes. Myths support creation-beliefs that can be conceived either as legends or as facts.

Legends are usually defined as a story with important ontological consequences passed from person to person. Legends are said to be ideal or semi-true story with mythic qualities usually involving a heroic character, a fantastic place, a sense of truth. The origin of the myths and legends of Chiloé is still uncertain.

As pointed out before, the first inhabitants of the island were Huilliches, even though some historians refer to them as Mapuches. Is is also said they were the same people who received different names according to the place they used to live. In this case, Mapuches is the general term used to refer to these people and Huilliches to those Mapuches living in the South.

Mapuche mythology can be explained in two different ways: the first one belonging to their own culture which shows the existence of evil and good gods; evil and good spirits; superstitions and magic. The other one mainly influenced by the Catholic concept of creation. The place where gods lived was called "Wenumapu"; the one in which men lived was named "Nagmapu". "Ranginapu" was a kind of intermediate land where the spirits of those who had recently died stayed a long time until they got the necessary knowledge to go live with their gods.

Mapuche religion is basically based on the worship of their ancestors. The name of this ancestor was "Pillán" and each clan had its own Pillán. As it was established before, "Wenumapu" was the god-land. There the Wenu family lived: Wenu-fucha(the elder), Wenu-kushe(woman), Wenu-weche (the young man), and Wenu-ulcha (the young lady).

But also there are some other holy figures such as "Toquinche" and "Huecuve". Toquinche was the good god who created living things by using clay. Huecuve or Gualiche was his brother. It is said that Huecuve decided to play a joke on his brother and when he saw some statues his brother had made he blew on them giving them life. These creatures were human beings. In this way humans came into existence.

Mapuche mythological characters present in Chilote folk tales.

Mapuche deities are not abstract but concrete. Their creed was basically fetishist, so they thought spirits possessed a material shape. Mapuches believed that spirits could live inside inanimate objects for a long time. They also said that they could take the shape of one living, strange, or fantastic creature to exist for a period of time.

Pillán: He was the god of thunder and lightening. He was in charge of giving fire. He also produced the volcanoe eruptions. It is said that when chiefs and warrios died in a battle their spirits became pillán. Chiefs became volcanoes and warriors became clouds.

Below is an extract from "Volcán de Villarica". It is a poem by Gabriela Mistral, Chile's first Nobel Prize winner, in which "Pillán" is mentioned:

Volcán de Villarica
by Gabriela Mistral
(pg. 207, **Poema de Chile**)

Entre resplandores y humos,
exorcismos olvidados,
la indiada secreta va
y viene, brazos en alto,
o se calla en piedra atónita,
en la compunción antigua:
porque el Pillán va cruzando
y la tierra araucana
reverbera de mirarlo,
viejo Pillán que gestea
con relámpagos y truenos.

*English Translation below:

Between flashes and smoke,
exorcisms forgotten,
indiada secret comes
and goes, arms raised,
or is silent in stunned stone,
in ancient compunction:
because the Pillán is crossing
and Araucarian land
reverberates to see him,
Old Pillán who gestures
with lightning and thunder.

Huecuvus: He could take different shapes to accomplish his evil instincts. Mapuches made him responsible for their sickness and some climatic changes.

Cherruves: He was a genius with the form of a snake having a human head. He was responsible for the appearance of comets. The Mapuches believed that the appearance of this creature brought them bad luck and disgrace.

Meuler: It was a kind of lizard that was believed to produce storms. When a storm began he hid inside the ground.

Auchimalgen: She was considered to be the spouse of the sun. She was a good god who protected people against evil spirits.

Huallipenyi: It was related to the appearance of fog. It has the body of a goat and the head of a cow. If a kid was born with any kind of physical malformation this creature was supposed to be responsible.

Chonchonyi: It was considered to be an evil spirit of inferior importance. It had the shape of a human head with big ears that helped it to fly long distances. Once he got to a place with sick people he waited until they were without company. Then it sucked their blood until it killed them.

Colo-Colo or Basilisco: This creature killed humans by sucking their saliva from them.

Pihuechenyi: It was a kind of vampire which sucked the blood from the sleepy Indians.

Mythological Chilote characters.

Before the arrival of the Huilliches to the island there was a peaceful group of natives:

Los Chonos:
Probably the mixture between this tribe and the Huilliches gave birth to the most amazing group of mythological characters. They are more earthly and share human characteristics.

La Pincoya: She is a woman who lives in the sea. She has long golden hair and wears a seaweed dress. It is said that when she was just a child she cried for a long time, so she became water. Huenchula, her mother, threw her into the ocean. In this way she became a woman. She rules fishing. It is said that if she is seen dancing in the ocean facing the land, fishermen are not going to have a god catch. On the contrary, if she is seen dancing facing the sea, fishermen will have good fishing. She also rescues those men who have gotten lost after a shipwreck taking them into the Caleuche.

El Trauco: He is a short man who lives in the woods of Chiloe. He is very aggressive with men and gentle with women. He exerts a sexual attraction on women. In fact, it is said that only his glancing can make a woman get pregnant.

La Fiura: She is Trauco's wife. She also exerts a sexual attraction on men. Once she has satisfied her desires, she gets their vital energy. This causes their death.

La Viuda (The widow): Even though she behaves in the same way La Fiura does, what makes the difference is that she does not kill the men. Nevertheless, if they refuse to accept her sexual requirements she kills them.

La Vaca Marina: This creature lives in the sea and feels special attraction towards bulls. When she sees one bull near the coast, she leaves the ocean and goes to catch it. Once there, she seduces it. When she thinks she has satisfied her natural instincts she goes back to the ocean.

El Camahueto: It is a powerful calf that has a silver horn in the middle of its forehead. The legend says that if a wizard can capture it under the light of the full moon and cut its horn, then he can prepare some secret poison used to alleviate sexual dysfunctions. In a way, it resembles the legend of the unicorn.

El Caleuche: It is a phantom ship that sails the seas and often appears in the Chiloe channels. El Caleuche sails on and under the surface of the sea. On calm nights it emerges through the fog, as a big sailing-ship that is beautifully lit. Music, voices and laughter can be heard. El Caleuche's crew is made of two kinds of sailors: wizards who enrich the trip riding "El Caballo Marino", and dead shipwrecked carried to the ship by La Pincoya. El Caleuche is under Millalobo orders.

Millalobo: He lives in the deepest sea. He is the son of a pretty woman and a seal. He is like a big seal, with a mix of man and fish face. The superior half of the body looks like a man, and the rest as a seal. His skin is covered by short and shining gold pelt. Its name means "gold wolf". He lives with "La Huenchula". Like a sea master, he gives some missions to several water creatures. He rules the growing and multiplication of sea creatures and controls the storms. He also commands the actions of evil creatures such as "La Vaca Marina". He has three children: La Pincoya, La Sirena, and El Pincoy.

El Pincoy: He is Millalobo's son. He has a big seal body and a beautiful human face. He is in charge of his father's domains.

El Caballo Marino: This creature is in charge of carrying either wizards or dead shipwrecked to El Caleuche.

La Huenchula: The only daughter of a married couple, she was pretty and gentle. Her duties were to carry water from the near lake to her house. One day, she began complaining about her obligations. She was not rejecting her duties but she manifested the horror she felt to realize that there was a strange creature watching her almost all the time. Her parents neither believed her nor paid attention to her words.

The next day, she was taken by this creature into the ocean. At her house her family was desperate. They looked for her day after day and they could not find her. Long after this, Huenchula appeared in their dreams. She told her parents she had married a powerful king who ruled the ocean. She also said she had come back to give them presents from her kingdom.

Her parents realized she was holding a creature in her arms. Just for a moment, she left this creature inside a vase. When Huenchula came back she noticed the creature had turned into water. This creature was her daughter and had the shape of a limpet. Feeling scared and sad, she took what was left from the creature and returned to the ocean where her husband was waiting for her.

Witchcraft

Chilote witchcraft has its origin in Europe. First, it was brought into the island by the Spanish settlers. Later on, new practices were held by colonizers from other regions of Europe. This fact and the pre-existing mythology had built a strong belief among locals who still talk about the presence of "brujos" (wizards) and "brujas" (witches).

Wizards and witches are said to be very powerful. They can fly taking a vertical position. They can also take on different animal shapes such as serpents, birds, and wild cats. They can hypnotize people and put evil spells on them. These spells usually cause sickness and death. Spells are denominated *maleficios* or *males*.

CHAPTER FOUR

EL TRAUCO & LA FIURA

Characters:

1. El Trauco: He is a short man who lives in the woods of Chiloe. He is very aggressive with men and gentle with women. He exerts a sexual attraction on women. In fact, it is said that by his only glancing for a fraction of a second at a woman, it is enough to make her become pregnant.

2. La Fiura: She is Trauco's wife. Similar to her husband, she also exerts a sexual attraction on men. Once she has satisfied her desires, she gets their vital energy. This causes the man's death.

3. Maria, a young, unmarried woman (19 years old)

4. José, a young, unmaried man (21 years old)

El Trauco: The Legend

AKA Trauco or Thrauco, this mythical being is described as a small man, no more than 80 cm. tall, with sharply defined manly features, an ugly face, yet having a very sweet look, alluring and sensual; no feet, as his legs end in stumps.

He wears a straw suit. His hat is also made of straw, pointed at the top, slopind down into a circular form. In his right hand he carries a stone ax, which transforms itself into a twisted cane (the Pahueldún) when he is standing in front of a girl.

Hanging from a hook on a sturdy tree branch, the Trauco waits for his unsuspecting victim: a young woman who is single.

When a young woman goes into the forest, the Trauco descends rapidly from his observation point, then gives three strong ax blows in the tree where he has been observing from. This is so loud that it seems to chop down all the trees.

When the girl is recovers from his surprise, she has the fascinating Trauco with her. He blows gently with his cane, the "Pahueldún". Without being able to resist, the young woman stares into the bright and devilish eyes of the Trauco, falling into a peaceful sleep of love.

After minutes, maybe hours, she wakes up angry and tearful. She is almost naked and her clothes are scattered around her. She shakes the grass and leaves quickly from her hair, fastenes her garments, and still somewhat dazed, heads back home.

As the months pass, the young woman's body is transformed, as she has been possessed by the Trauco. At nine months the son of Trauco is born.

This fact does not socially affect neither the child nor his mother, because now both are related to the mysterious, magical, mythical Trauco.

**

La Fiura: The Legend

La Fiura looks like a small woman with an ugly face, long hair, full breasts, thin and hooked fingers and toes. She is usually wearing a short, red skirt. Habitually, she suddenly takes on capricious and convulsive postures. She makes horrible facial expressions with her ugly face and sparkling eyes, which are almost hidden by a huge nose. She extends her arms in all directions and twitches the deformed fingers of her huge hands, looking for a victim to "throw an air".

You can see her dancing on the delicate forest carpet, a soft bog, without fear that at any instant, the soft landmass under her feet will break and the swamp will swallow her whole. Occasionally, she ceases to dance, in order to observe her ugly face in the reflection of a puddle and comb her hair with a shiny silver comb.

Coquettishly shaking her prominent breasts, she runs nimbly between the logs burned by the friction of her dancing. Waving her short red skirt, she moves her arms and legs agilely among the semi-carbonized tree branches.

Then, she sneaks into the bushes, looking for the spiny "chauras", eating greedily. The slightest noise scares her easily.

The Fiura, only daughter of "La Condená", is the wife of the virile Trauco. However, this fact does not stop her from offering her love to all men. She demands of her men one condition. They must accept her unseen, that is to say, with their eyes blindfolded.

She does not allow even a glimpse of herself, not even that of animals. The brave ones, who dare to look at her, become twisted somewhere in their body. If the beholder is a child or an animal, their legs become deformed, making it impossible to walk.

Fight with her? No, it is impossible. She possesses such strength and skill, that not even the strongest men can overcome her. She leaves them battered and bruised all over, trembling from the exertion. As much as you try to hit her, she receives not a single blow, it's like trying to hit a shadow.

The deformations caused by Fiura are practically incurable except fortunate cases, in which by the following treatment can get relief:

At dawn a branch of the vine called "Pahueldún" is cut. Once transported by the ill, whips the branch until the sap runs from the Pahueldún. The sap must be drunk the sick person. Then the branch is the dragged to the beach, where it is thrown into the sea. It is also said that you could take scrapings from the "Ara Stone" to counter the evils caused by Fiura.

**

CHAPTER FIVE

Delightful Dreams

María Jesús, a very pretty young woman of 19 years was sleeping in her bed in Ancud. She was dreaming the same dream again, a delightfully delicious dream that she had told nobody about. How could she?

She had been having a dream of a handsome man with an amazing look in his eyes, taking her by the hand and leading her to a place in the forest that was quiet and secluded. Mmm, she felt warm all over, tingling sensations running all through her body. Every morning, the evidence of her intense feelings while she had the dream had been visible on her bedsheets.

Outside her window, a weird looking man peered inside at her. Hanging from a large branch he had an unobstructed view inside her room. Tonight the moon would be full. Tonight.

The sound of the rooster crowing announced a new day had dawned. He must leave this place, for he did not wish to be seen. That would complicate things, and the last thing El Trauco wanted at this stage of his plans was complications.

Meanwhile, José was up early, as usual. When the rooster crowed, it was time to get up, wash his face, have his breakfast and make his way to his boat. José was a young man of 21 years. He was tall, rugged, and strong. Since the age of 14, he had been going to fish alone. It was his daily catch that provided food and income for him and his grandmother, Ana.

Ever since his parents had died when he was only six years old,

Ana had taken care of him as best as she could. She was a wise woman, who lived frugally, and had managed to ensure that José always had a warm bed to sleep in, a full stomach, and all the love she could give him. He was her life, but she knew the time had come for him to find a partner to share his life with.

The first time he mentioned María Jesús, she had said nothing. Since then, Ana had watched her carefully. She was a good girl, strong, hard-working, and she attended church regularly. After assuring herself that María would make a fine wife for José, she had encouraged him to stop by her house to see if there was anything he could do to help her and her grandfather, Pedro.

As time had gone by, the two had become good friends. They talked with one another whenever they could, and would often visit for a short while in the morning when José passed by on his way to his fishing boat in the early hours of the morning.

But Ana felt that something was wrong. José had been quiet for two days now, and last night, he had finally told her that he had not seen María recently. It seems she was sleeping longer nowadays.

Ana had lived in Ancud all her life. Although life in the city was not as mysterious as life in the interior of the island, she knew all the mysteries and superstitions of her people. Indeed, she had been a young girl once, and she knew that sweet dreams for young girls on this island were dangerous dreams. She would visit Pedro today, and there were two things she were taking with her to Mariá's house.

As José went past Mari´s house, he saw her grandfather cutting firewood with his ax. Pedro was also an early riser, and he had often did chores with the help of José and María early in the morning. There was wood to chop, chickens to feed, cows to milk, and water to carry back into the house all before he took his breakfast. The three of them usually finished these tasks very quickly, but with María still sleeping in bed, it was slower.

"Don Pedro, for days now I have not seen María in the morning. Is everything....?"

His voice trailed off. Pedro looked at him quietly before answering. Choosing his words carefully, he said, "You are quite fond of her, aren't you?

Without waiting for an answer, he continued. The look in José's eyes had told him everything. Soon, there would be a wedding to prepare. But first, he would have to have a talk with Ana. Ana, she had never forgiven him for marrying Susana. But Susana had needed him more than Ana had. Pedro had made his decision, and whenever he looked at María, he knew he had made the right decision.

So long ago, almost 19 years to the day, Susana had left the house early and gone into the forest to find fire wood. He had come by to see her, just as José had come by to see María. When he didn't find her in the yard, he had not been concerned. He had gone on his way down to the harbor to go to his fishing boat.

La Pincoya had been seen early that morning, looking out to the sea. It would be a long journey to an alternate fishing ground. To make time, he had cut through the forest, something he never did. No Chilote ever went through the forest early in the morning after a full moon, for spirits and creatures from other worlds were said to inhabit the forest.

He had not gone far when Pedro had seen the back of a woman. She had long hair, flaming in the rays of the earliest sunlight of the day. "Susana?"

Her back was turned to him but she said nothing. He came closer, and she began dancing sensually, her hips moving from side to side, her hair waving in the wind that suddenly began to blow as if she had commanded it.

She held out her hand to him, shyly, and whispered, "Cover your eyes with this. You must not see me."

He obeyed instantly, without knowing why he liked this game so much, for he and Susana had never played like this before. With the blindfold over his eyes securely, he could see nothing, but he could feel Susana. Her feminine softness was pressed to his body, and he lost all thoughts of going fishing. There in the forest, they joined together. It was exquisite, like nothing he had ever experienced before. He drifted away into a sweet, delightful sleep, dreaming of Susana and him.

A loud piercing scream awoke him. Looking around him, he found himself alone. Again, the anguished scream came from the forest. He ran quickly, and there he found Susana lying at the foot of a tree. She was nearly naked, and her clothes were in disarray all around her. It looked as if she had been seduced, had made love hurriedly, and upon waking, had found herself all alone.

He tried to reassure her. "Susana, let me help you. Everything is all right. I am here with you, I never left you. You must have wandered away from me."

Susana looked at him curiously. "You never left me. I never left you either."

Up above them, in the tree, two strange creatures looked down on them. There was a very short man, and a very ugly woman. The short man was wearing a cone shaped hat, and carried an ax in his right hand. In the other, a twisted cane was evident. The ugly woman was wearing a short red skirt, had long hair, and a look of intense satisfaction on her face.

With her clothes neatly arranged, the two had walked together back to Susana's house. That very morning Pedro had proposed marriage to Susana, and she had accepted.

It had been the least Pedro could do, having taken Susana's honor in the forest. They set the date as quickly as possible, knowing that which is done in the dark of night would soon come to the light of day.

In the months that followed, the changes in Susana's body were noticeable. Nine months later, María Jesús was born. Unfortunately, Susana died from complications during delivery, as she had been in labor a very long time, and the loss of blood had been severe.

Pedro had raised María Jesús from her birth up to the present day, sacrificing his life to ensure that she had everything he could possibly give her.

"Sir?", repeated José for the third time. He took him by the shoulder and gently shook him.

Pedro came back from his reverie. He had a far away look in his eye. "You are fond of María Jesús, aren't you?

"Yes, I am."

"You must come by tonight, after you return from your fishing today. I want to have a talk with you and María. Go now. Hurry, or you will get started too late to have a good catch today. Off with you, my son."

As José hurried away, a tear rolled slowly down his cheek. It had been the first time that the old man had ever called him, "Son". Wiping the tear away with his sleeve, he went on his way.

CHAPTER SIX

Trinity

"Are you sure, Ana?" asked Pedro. "Is it him?

"Yes, it is him, and he is not alone. She is with him."

"But how can you be so sure? Have you seen them?"

"They are here. I have not seen them. To look at them is to risk your life. But, their signs are everywhere. María can not arise early because her dreams are delightful and sweet. The sounds of animals passing by are heard, but there are no animals. The sounds coming from the forest are unnaturally quiet. They are here I tell you."

"I could not bear to lose María Jesús."

"And I could not bear to lose my José."

The silence hung heavy between them as the thought of losing their loved ones was unthinkable, causing them both pain. At long last Pedro asked Ana, "What are we going to do?"

"There are three things we must tell them. Never look at them, not even for a moment. Never touch them, and if they do get close to them, never breathe in their breath."

"Yes, that is important. And María must never go into the forest alone. Someone must always be with her whenever she leaves this house."

"Then he will come here looking for her. He already sends his delightful dreams to her. He seems to know he will have to come here to get her, and already he has a plan. We must be very careful Pedro, or we will lose them both."

Ana took out a bottle of fine sand she had gathered on the beach before coming here to visit Pedro.

"What's this?" asked Pedro.

"Sand", said Ana. "Don't you want to count each grain of sand?"

Pedro rolled his eyes at her and spoke sharply, "Of course not. Get serious woman. We are talking about the lives of our children here."

Ana smiled. "I am serious. Although YOU may not want to count each grain of sand in this jar, HE will. And as he counts each grain of sand, the night will slip away, and when day breaks, he must be away from here."

"Clever, very clever Ana. You are well informed I see. You have talked to the Machi. What else can we do?

Again Ana reached into her bag. She drew out this time two knives. Crossing them, she handed them to Pedro. "As long as these knives are crossed and in Maria´s room, he will not be able to enter. Cross the knives, and he enters not."

Pedro nodded his head. He looked at her expectantly. Surely she had more tricks up her sleeve.

Wordlessly, she reached her hand into her bag, and pulled out a small hand ax. She rose, and walked outside. Pedro followed her. Walking to each corner of the house, she hacked it in turn. Finishing, they walked back inside. No words had passed between them.

"And now?", asked Pedro.

"In this house, he will not come. María is safe here, inside. She is in danger when she leaves this house, and if she ever goes into the forest, he will get her."

"Am I to be a prisoner in this house until I am an old lady?" asked María. She came out from behind the door where she had been listening to them talking.

"What did you hear, my child?", asked Ana.

"Everything", said Ana. "You have explained everything that has been happening to me recently."

"María, if you are ever followed by this man, do not look at him. RUN! Run to the ocean, and get in a boat. Row far out to the sea," said Ana.

"But he will catch me, won't he?"

"No", said Ana. You are taller and much faster than he. With his short legs, he will never catch you in a foot race. But he will never give up, and that is why you must run to a boat and row out to sea."

"He will catch me in the water when I get tired, then." María dropped her head in resignation. "I am doomed."

"No, my child. María, look at me. He can not swim."

Pedro lifted his head when he heard that. "Does José know that?"

"Yes, he does my friend." "He also knows to trust nobody who speaks to him outside, not you, not me, not María, nobody. Outside, the only safety is the sea."

And now Pedro stood up, and looked at Ana. Opening the jar of sand, he told María to always carry sand with her. If any man were to follow her, throw sand at him.

Ana nodded her head. "Yes, if you leave this house, always carry sand with you. Good Pedro, you have understood."

Ana watched as Pedro went to the fireplace and removed ashes. Going to each corner of each room, he placed ashes there.

Again Ana nodded her head. "Yes, there is no entry into this house for him. You are safe here."

María turned to go, but Ana said, "Wait. Don't go yet. Tell me about your dreams."

"No, I can not do that. Those dreams are too..."

Her voice trailed away. It was impossible for her to speak of the dreams of love and passion she had been having.

"María", said Ana firmly, "when you speak of the deams, they lose their power over you."

With her cheeks burning a bright red, she sat down and began to speak of the dreams. She felt herself relaxing, the tension leaving her body as she spoke of the handsome man who had been a part of her dreams every night, and of the feelings the dreams had provoked within her...

CHAPTER SEVEN

Chonchi & Quellón
Months passed by. With each passing month, María, José, Pedro,

and Ana felt safer. Someone in Ancud mentioned that a young woman was expecting a child in Chonchi. Another said it wasn't Chonchi, it was Quellón. At any rate, both Chonchi and Quellón, located in the center and extreme south of the island, were far away from Ancud. It seemed El Trauco had given up on María.

Nonetheless, José continued to go everywhere with garlic rubbed on his palm. Not only did it keep La Fiura far away from him, but it also kept El Trauco far away from him. And he constantly had a pair of swiss knives crossed in his pocket, not to mention the sand he carried around with him.

By now, Ana was sure of one thing. If El Trauco still entertained any hope of bewitching and trapping María, it would come through José. Ana knew El Trauco had virtually no power over María's dreams, and if it dared to enter the house, he would have no chance of success. No, the weak link was the relationship between José and María.

The only thing Ana was not sure about was La Fiura, the wife of El Trauco. They had once worked together to trick Pedro into thinking he had been the one responsible for Susana.

When she heard the story about Susana's pregnancy, she had known Pedro was not responsible. He was a good man, with a good heart, but Susana had no feelings for him. Ana knew because Susana had told her she did not fancy him. Ana had been so happy to hear those words from her friend.

But when Ana found out what happened to Susana and Pedro in the forest, she knew she would never get any one of them to accept the truth. Both had faced the reality of their situation as she would have done under similar circumstances. Susana needed a husband, and a father, for her child. Pedro's sense of honor had made him the perfect sacrifice. That could be the only reason El Trauco and La Fiura had allowed him to live, to take care of their child.

And now they were back, to further torment him. It was not enough what they had done to his life. No, now they wanted his very soul. To do that, all they had to do was subject María to the same treatment they had subjected Susana to. It would drive Pedro mad, over the brink of insanity.

What to do? Hadn't she done all that she could to keep everyone safe? Inside of her, a little voice whispered to her, "NO. You haven't done all that you can."

Inhaling deeply, she knew that she must somehow kill Trauco and his wife. Only then would innocent lives not be sacrificed to the immorality and destruction that this ungodly couple reveled in, lived for, and would surely, die for?

Yes, that unholy couple would surely die for a chance to work their evil. Ana had found their weakness, but she knew that she would have to offer the one person in this world who she loved more than anything, José.

The stakes were high. Life or death, eternal peace or eternal damnation. Looking at her figure of the Virgin Mary, she wondered if she would be strong enough to do what she knew she had to do.

CHAPTER EIGHT

Hail Mary

Tonight. Tonight would be the night. Again, the moon was full. And again, José would meet María outside, just as they had the last three nights. Only tonight, José would not be wearing any garlic on his hands. He would not be carrying his Swiss knives crossed in his pocket. He would have no sand. He would be defenseless. If anything went wrong, his life would be sacrificed. Again, Ana prayed to the Virgin Mary.

Hail Mary

Hail Mary, full of grace, the Lord is with thee!
Blessed art thou among women, and blessed is the fruit of thy womb, Jesus.
Holy Mary, Mother of God, pray for us sinners, now and at the hour of our death. Amen.

Then they all saw José walking toward the house. He was alone, and walking, coming closer, but was it him? Pedro looked at her, María looked at her. Was it him? Is it José?

With her heart tearing apart, Ana stod motionless. A cold chill ran down her spine. José had not made the agreed upon sign. María could not leave the house. That man outside was looking expectantly at the window, where they were all watching for a sign from him which never came.

José was dead. Trauco had killed him, or La Fiura. Did it matter who killed him, or how he had died? Silent tears ran down her cheeks, slowly at first, and then the tears flowed like a raging river that would not be stopped.

Pedro and María hugged her tightly, embracing to share equally in the pain. They had all lost something precious, something special. Whose loss was greater?

María had lost a husband. María had lost the father of her future children. Her life would go on. She had promised José she would live if she ever lost him.

Pedro had lost a friend. Pedro had lost a son-in-law. His life would go on. As long as María was alive, Pedro would live. She was his reason for living.

Ana? Ana's life was over. José was all that she had in this world. She had raised him, watched him grow up into a strong, loving son. Son? Yes, he was more her son than grandson, for she had been mother and father to him. Their bond was deeper than any umbilical cord could ever have made it.

She raised her eyes to look outside one more time. The moon had gone behind some clouds and she saw clearly the outline of two figures, one a hideously deformed, short man, ax in his right hand, cane in his left.

Beside him was a woman wearing a short skirt, her back turned to the house. Even now, at this distance, the powerful charms of the house were keeping La Fiura back, not even allowing her to look at the house in the darkness.

Ana smiled. At least, the magic protecting the house was powerful. And then she saw it.

"Look! It's José!" Amazed, Pedro and María looked on.

Outside, "La Fiura" had taken the twisted cane, the Pahueldún, and was dragging it in the dirt as he ran for the ocean. As he dragged the Pahueldún, José beat it again and again upon the ground, bringing it down fiercely, trying to break it.

Each time he did that, El Trauco felt the blows to his body as if he had been physically struck. His body contorted again and again with each blow José applied to the cane. Swiftly he ran, easily outdistancing the agonising Trauco.

Arriving at the ocean, he got into his rowboat. As he rowed out, he dragged the cane in the water. The Trauco was being drowned! As the stick was under water, so was the Trauco! Reaching deeply into the harbor, José sank the Pahueldún into the water, dropping it over the side tied to a weight designed to keep it down beneath the water for a hnded years if need be...

El Trauco drowned that night...

María and José lived happily ever after, the only Chilotes I know who fought with El Trauco, and lived to tell the tale of his defeat.

The End

ABOUT THE AUTHOR

Thomas Baker is the Past-President of TESOL Chile

(2010-2011).

Thomas is also a past member of the Advisory Board for the International Higher Education Teaching and Learning Association (HETL), where he also serves as a reviewer and as the HETL Ambassador for Chile.

Thomas enjoys writing about a wide variety of topics. He has written the following genres: romance, mythology, historical fiction, autobiography, sports history, biography, and English Language Teaching.

Author Page on Amazon:
https://www.amazon.com/author/thomasjeromebaker

Printed in Great Britain
by Amazon.co.uk, Ltd.,
Marston Gate.